Discovering
The Gospel
According to YOU

A BASIC PRIMER ON
THEOLOGICAL EXPLORATION

Allen E Henninger MDiv

WESTBOW
PRESS®
A DIVISION OF THOMAS NELSON
& ZONDERVAN

This book is a work of non-fiction. Unless otherwise noted, the author
and the publisher make no explicit guarantees as to the accuracy of
the information contained in this book and in some cases, names of
people and places have been altered to protect their privacy.

WestBow Press books may be ordered through booksellers or by contacting:

WestBow Press
A Division of Thomas Nelson & Zondervan
1663 Liberty Drive
Bloomington, IN 47403
www.westbowpress.com
844-714-3454

Because of the dynamic nature of the Internet, any web addresses or
links contained in this book may have changed since publication and
may no longer be valid. The views expressed in this work are solely those
of the author and do not necessarily reflect the views of the publisher,
and the publisher hereby disclaims any responsibility for them.

Unless otherwise noted, scripture quotations taken from the (NASB®) New
American Standard Bible®, Copyright © 1960, 1971, 1977, 1995, 2020 by The
Lockman Foundation. Used by permission. All rights reserved. www.lockman.org

Scripture marked (KJV) taken from the King James Version of the Bible.

Scripture quotations marked (RSV) are from Revised Standard Version of the Bible,
copyright © 1946, 1952, and 1971 National Council of the Churches of Christ in
the United States of America. Used by permission. All rights reserved worldwide.

ISBN: 978-1-6642-8248-3 (sc)
ISBN: 978-1-6642-8249-0 (e)

Library of Congress Control Number: 2022919983

Print information available on the last page.

WestBow Press rev. date: 02/02/2023

We are an epistle, not written with ink but by the Spirit of God. (2 Corinthians 3:2-3), and that's at the heart of Allen Henninger's book, *Discovering the Gospel According to You*. I've been friends with Allen for a few decades now, which I realize that by saying so is a bit like carbon dating our friendship. But this long friendship gives has given me a bird's-eye view of his life and ministry.

I've seen Allen in the pulpit, both as a visiting speaker to churches I've pastored, and in churches where he was the pastor. I have seen him in coffeehouses with people who did not share his own faith, and in festivals where the world arrived to party and try to find meaning outside of faith. I've seen Allen navigate tragedy and come out the other side stronger. In these things, he has been an example for me. Together we watched church leadership become abusive and we've both suffered through that abuse. Allen was one of those people who were there for me in my struggles.

I rehearse this history to make a point: Allen is an example of what he writes about. He is generous, supportive, intelligent, and most of all--he is all about the gospel. He is an epistle of love wrapped in a rough and humorous cover.

Many endorsements are written by people who barely know the writer, consequently, there are warehouses of Christian books written by people who are not good examples and shouldn't be telling us how to live. Allen knows what he is talking about, and his life models what he shares. Read, learn, grow and allow the gospel according to Allen help you in *Discovering the Gospel According to You.*

Phil Wyman
Author of *Burning Religion: navigating the impossible space between religion and secular society*

Don't be alarmed by the title. Allen Henninger makes a biblically solid case I had never seen before. We are the gospel lived out to those around us. They'll be drawn to The Book only if they first see The Book lived out in <u>us</u>.

Mr. Henninger takes us on a refreshing and exciting journey to discover the truth of what we believe. This book is the door that beckons us to that journey.

I was encouraged to stop "just reading" the Bible, and start experiencing it on a deeper level. Mr. Henninger gives us the tools to go digging for treasure.

His key verse is Psalm 119:18: "Open my eyes, that I may behold wonderful things from Your law." This book will open your eyes. Get ready for wonderful things.

John Fornof,
Writer-Director-Producer
Circle Creative Media

Discovering The Gospel According to You is a very straightforward exposure to the Christian Life and sets forth realistic concepts of witnessing where most people have just had to toss a coin, scratch their head, take a deep breath, and do their best. It gives Christians specifics to look for in scripture to find out what they really believe, and how to effectively share those beliefs with others.

Definitely a great book, non-pretentious, and not too wordy or pseudo-intellectual. I highly recommend it.

Jim Kruger,
Vice President / Loan Officer
Kruger Investment Company
Oklahoma City, Oklahoma

Dedication

This book is dedicated to the many wonderful, patient, and encouraging mentors and friends who have been great examples to me of smart and learned followers of Christ.

Thanks to them, I have discovered my version of *The Gospel According to You.*

Introduction

During my tenure as a missionary, I spent many hours talking to people about Jesus, attempting to influence them toward following Christ. I gradually begin to see that most of these people were not interested in knowing about the Gospel according to Matthew, Mark, Luke, or John; they wanted to learn about the Gospel according to Allen.

If you are a committed Christian who wants to fulfill the commandment "Go into all the world and preach the Gospel to all Creation" (Mark 16:15), you must have a competent knowledge of what you believe the good news about Jesus is. You should arrive at your own understanding of who He is and what His plan is for us humans and all of his creation. Then you will be able to more efficiently tell others "the gospel according to you."

This book was written for those who are or want to be disciples of Christ. In the original Greek of the New Testament, the word that we get *disciple* from means "learner." I am writing to Christians who want to learn of Him and from Him. I hope that's you!

I also want to stress that unless you are living a holy life, your pursuit of "the gospel according to you" is futile. God only tells His deep truths to those who are living in obedience to Him and His Word. He also only tells His mysteries to those who care to know.

Please be advised that in this book, I'm not saying that you should develop a whole new religion or depart from sound Biblical doctrine with your unique presentation of the Gospel. Rather I'm asking that you diligently search after what you believe about Christ and His Kingdom. Then, take your message to those who desperately need to hear it.

That being said, as we embark on this exciting journey of discovering truth, I am reminded of the parable of the blind men and an elephant. It is a story of a group of blind men who had never encountered an elephant and learn and imagine what the elephant is like by touching it. Each blind man feels a different part of the elephant's body, but only one part, such as the side or the tusk, ear, or trunk. They then describe the elephant based on their limited experience and their descriptions of the elephant are different from each other.

This is a good illustration of Christian beliefs; we have essential doctrines that must be adhered to if we want to claim that we are Christians. These are

1. The deity of Christ (Jesus is God);
2. Salvation by grace (not by works); and
3. The resurrection of Christ (Jesus rose from the dead).

However, there are many different ways of understanding these beliefs. For example, how did Christ's death enable the forgiveness of our sins? What does it mean that Christ is Lord over all? This book's purpose is to help you figure out what you understand about these concepts and to confirm that you actually believe them.

Scripture tells us that we are to be stewards of the mysteries of God. As stated in 1 Corinthians 4:1, "Let a man regard us in this manner, as servants of Christ and stewards of the mysteries of God." This is the challenge to us: discover these mysteries and pass them on in our own words and ways.

It is my hope and prayer that, as you pursue this wonderful journey into truth, it will not be a laborious or boring one. I hope it will help you develop a deeper personal understanding of, and relationship with, our great God, which will be invigorating and exciting.

Getting Started

The first four books of the New Testament are called the Gospels. Here's what the *Encyclopedia Brittanica* has to say about the word *gospel*.

> The word *gospel* is derived from the Anglo-Saxon term *god-spell*, meaning "good story," a rendering of the Latin *evangelium* and the Greek *euangelion*, meaning "good news" or "good telling."[1]

The purpose of each of the authors (Matthew, Mark, Luke, and John) of the Gospels was to tell the "good news" of the coming of the Messiah, Jesus Christ. Yet each delivered his own unique, and accurate, presentation of the Gospel. You too should be able to present a unique presentation of the truths of the Christian Gospel. This is what I call "the gospel according to you."

This phrase "the gospel according to you" may sound strange to you, but even the apostle Paul uses the phrase " according to my Gospel" in two separate verses: 2 Timothy 2:8 and Romans 2:16. The apostle Paul serves as

---

[1] "Gospel," Brittanica, last updated December 7, 2018, https://www. britannica.com/topic/Gospel-New-Testament.

good example for us. He discovered His gospel, and it's time for us to discover ours.

To further define what the "gospel according to you" is, let me use a personal illustration of how "the gospel according to Allen" came in handy when I was witnessing to someone a few years ago:

Back then I was involved in an outreach on the east coast and was asked to play bass in a band that was being formed out of the outreach participants, We had enough musicians for a band except we didn't have a drummer. So, A local pastor had a friend whom he asked to play with us, and we were able to pull it off. However, I soon found out that our drummer, who had graciously volunteered to play with us, was not a follower of Christ. As we began playing together, the drummer and I had an almost immediate rapport and began spending a lot of time together. As we continued getting to know each other, I discovered that his family growing up had been less than idyllic, to say the least, and wished that it had been different. As he was sharing this with me, I felt the Holy Spirit prompting me to tell him about the relational nature of the trinity that I learned about by reading a book entitled; *The Ultimate Intention*[2], by DeVern Fromke. In this book, the author shares that the Father, is desiring a family, The Son is desiring a bride and The Holy Spirit is desiring a temple in which to dwell. I shared with my new friend that by giving his life to Christ he would become an immediate participant in all three of these wonderful relationships. I particularly emphasized that he would be a part of a

---

[2] DeVern, Fromke, *The Ultimate Intention,* Sure Foundation,1963

new family. And one that is not dysfunctional, like his earthly one.

My friend told me he had never heard these concepts before and it seemed to birth a desire in him to learn more about God. My friend did not make a commitment to Christ that day, and I had to return to my home in California shortly thereafter. But, the local pastor, who has an ongoing friendship with him, tells me that his interest in Christ has been revitalized since our conversation.

Because I had applied myself to know about Christ, I was able to uniquely make him known that day. I didn't have to use a script written by someone else, I was able to tailor a very relevant message about our great God to my friend that day. I used "the gospel according to Allen" that day.

So "the Gospel according to you" can be defined as; your unique understanding of God's plan to redeem every human, out of their sin and back to Him. This understanding can be discovered by spending much time getting to know Jesus, by consistently studying his word, meditating on it, and praying daily.

To that end, let us begin. However, be forewarned: developing a comprehensive and consistent gospel understanding involves a lot of time spent "being diligent to present yourself approved to God" (2 Timothy 2:12a).

To help you in the pursuit of your unique gospel, this book focuses on the four main areas outlined in what is known as the Wesleyan Quadrilateral. This is the system for theological reflection used by John Wesley, the founder of the Methodist Church. The term itself was developed by Albert C. Outler, a twentieth-century American Methodist scholar.

This method uses four different sources of theological reflection and doctrinal development. They are

1. scripture;
2. tradition;
3. experience; and
4. reason.

We will be exploring these four sources and more as we press forward in our quest for the gospel according to you. Let's begin.

Scripture

The Bible is the most important and authoritative source of truth and wisdom for Christians. All theological theories must be tested against scripture and found to be consistent with what it says. Therefore, it is the most important source of the four listed above.

The Bible does not contain God's word; it is God's written word to humans. It is a love letter written to guide his children through life.

The Bible is not a science book, but it is always accurate when it touches on science. It is not a music manual, yet it contains many songs. Scripture touches on many subjects, but its main purpose is to show us what God is like and what his plan is to reconcile all things to himself.

Before pursuing your study of scripture, it is important to know about "The Science and Art of Biblical

Interpretation."[3] Here we find helpful principles to help us arrive at a correct understanding of any given passage.

First, the ultimate goal of scriptural study is to understand what the original author was trying to say to the original audience. Why was the author writing what he or she was writing? What's the context?

What Dr. David L. Cooper calls the "Golden Rule of Interpretation" comes in handy here: "When the plain sense of scripture makes common sense, seek no other sense, therefore take every word at its primary, ordinary, usual, literal meaning unless the facts of the immediate context, studied in light of reality, dictate otherwise."[4]

For instance, Matthew 18:8 states,

> If your hand or foot causes you to stumble,
> cut it off and throw it from you; it is better
> for you to enter life crippled or lame than
> to have two hands or two feet and be cast
> into the eternal fire.

It's obvious, using the rule above, that this verse is not to be followed literally; however, Jesus is making the point that offenses using your hand or foot (murder, stealing, and so on) are serious sins in His eyes.

Jesus again reiterates the seriousness of sin in the next

---

[3] William L. Kynes, "The Science and Art of Interpretation," *How to Read the Bible,* podcast audio, March 27, 2021, https://www.cslewisinstitute. org/resources/knowing-doing-podcast-how-to-read-the-bible-part-2- the-science-and-art-of-interpretation/.

[4] Dr. David L. Cooper, "The Golden Rule of Interpretation," *Hermeneutics: The Science of Interpreting the Scriptures,* The Association of Messianic Congregations, accessed October 19, 2022, http://www. messianicassociation.org/ezine19-dc.hermeneutics.htm.

verse, this time using the eyes. Using common sense, in light of reality, we know He's not talking about the act of seeing; He's talking about lusting or coveting. The literal translation in these passages doesn't seem to be the right one in light of the aforementioned rule.

Context

Looking at the context of a passage is very important. Context is defined as "the parts of something written or spoken that immediately precede and follow a word or passage and clarify its meaning."[5] In other words, where the passage is found helps define what a particular word or group of words means.

For example, Philippians 4:13 is often quoted out of context. Let's look at this verse as it is often used: "I can do all things through Him who strengthens me." Now let's look at the entire passage from Bible:

> But I rejoiced in the Lord greatly, that now, at last, you have revived your concern for me; indeed, you were concerned before, but you lacked opportunity. Not that I speak from want, for I have learned to be content in whatever circumstances I am. I know how to get along with humble means, and I also know how to live in

[5] "Context," Oxford Learner's Dictionaries, accessed October 19, 2022, https://www.oxfordlearnersdictionaries.com/us/definition/english/context.

prosperity; in any and every circumstance I have learned the secret of being filled and going hungry, both of having abundance and suffering in need. I can do all things through Him who strengthens me. Nevertheless, you have done well to share with me my affliction. (Philippians 4:10–14)

If one reads this passage in context, it appears that Paul says he can do all *these* things through Christ who strengthens Him. I believe this is the correct understanding of this passage based upon the context.

When studying context, there are three important things to consider about the text.

1. Who was the original audience?
2. How does it relate to the larger narrative of the Bible?
3. How does it interact with the local portion of scripture where it is situated?

Word Study

Word study comes in handy here. A word's meaning in its original language is often very enlightening. To find the original meaning of a word, you will need to use reference books. Some helpful ones are *Vine's Expository Dictionary*, *Strong's Concordance*, *Manners and Customs of the Bible*, a parallel Bible, a Bible dictionary, and other Bible-related study tools.

When you look up the definition of words in the original language using the tools I mentioned, you will find that there is often more than one corresponding English word listed. This again illustrates the need to use context, common sense, reason, and other peoples' understanding to figure out which corresponding English word fits best.

Here's an example (a very controversial one, by the way).

> "You have heard that it was said, 'You shall not commit adultery;' but I say to you that everyone who looks at a woman with lust for her has already committed adultery with her in his heart." (Matthew 5:27–28)

Here we have a verse that has caused much needless pain for many Christian men throughout the ages because of the wrong interpretation of the word *lust*. If we do some in-depth word study here, we find that the word for "lust" in this passage has an alternate meaning: "covet." To commit adultery, one of the two parties involved needs to be married. Therefore, a better translation seems to be, "You have heard it said, 'You shall not commit adultery;' but I say to you that everyone who looks at his neighbor's wife to covet her has already committed adultery in his heart."

In addition, if we look at the context of this passage, we will find that Jesus seems to be reiterating the sixth, seventh, and tenth commandments here. Our passage emphasizes the tenth: "Thou shall not covet your neighbor's wife." Therefore, it seems that "covet" is the better translation of this word in this verse.

Although this understanding of this verse is not in line with its traditional interpretation, if we are to be true to the "Golden Rule of Interpretation," this seems to be the correct interpretation of this verse.

Let the Bible Interpret the Bible

All the methods that already mentioned are very useful in our interpreting process. However, there is no better interpreting tool than the Bible itself. When you are seeking to get a Biblical understanding of a particular topic, it's important to look at all the verses that deal with that topic to arrive at an understanding consistent with all of them.

Translations

It is also helpful when hunting for a correct understanding of a passage or verse to look at the many Bible translations available to us to see how these verses are translated there. Of course, some are reputed to be more accurate to the original language, such as the New American Standard Version. Others, such as the New International Version, are supposed to accurately convey the original author's thoughts. I find consulting as many versions as possible helpful in figuring out what the author is trying to convey in any given passage.

Beyond the Bible

As we pursue the true gospel two thousand years after scripture was written, we will encounter situations in this modern world that scripture doesn't directly address. What do we do then? We will pursue an answer to that question in our chapter on reason.

CHAPTER 12

Tradition

Although scripture should be the main source of truth in our Christian lives and theological development, we should also take into consideration the ideas and understanding of those who have gone before us in this quest to find the true gospel. In this modern age, we have access to a massive amount of resources to find out what others have thought about the scriptures and God. We should use them.

Is it important to know what gospel Paul, the apostle, preached? Of course. But how about what St. Augustine, Martin Luther, or John Wesley taught about Christ? Getting a grasp on what these great saints of God believed is essential to discover the gospel according to you.

Biblical commentaries are a good source of what others think about any given passage. Christian history books are also useful in finding out what those who have gone before us thought about our Christian faith.

In addition to personal beliefs, corporate (i.e., denominational) understandings of the good news about Jesus are important to consider. For instance, Mennonites believe Jesus was a pacifist; other denominations don't. Most Presbyterians believe that your salvation was predestined to happen before the creation of the earth, while others believe it must be freely received now. What do you think? It's very important to figure out what you confidently believe about these matters when developing your gospel.

These spiritual heroes of the past are important sources of understanding, but their views should not be adopted without thorough investigation on your part. How do you know what they believed and taught was and is true? You can only do this through study and prayer.

On the other hand, if you were raised in a specific Christian tradition, it's important to not adopt what you learned growing up without investigating the truth of what you were taught at that time. Let's face it: we want to believe that what we were taught by our Sunday school teachers, camp counselors, or pastors is true. However, since all of us are fallible, we need to be careful about adopting what we have heard without personally investigating it ourselves. Again, we need to be convinced that what we believe is what we are sure is the true understanding of the Gospel.

Convinced but Curious

To reiterate, I believe it's also a good practice to be curious about all opposing views to our currently held beliefs. After all, we are all finite people and prone to mistakes in our reasoning. It's good practice to investigate someone else's understanding of God, who He is, and how He works. However, in order to be considered a Christian, and have a gospel that is considered a Christian one, we must hold to certain beliefs. Let's explore these next.

The Traditional Essentials

Tradition has provided us with guidance in deciding the beliefs necessary to call your gospel a Christian one.

First, there is one God, manifest in three persons: Father, Son, and Holy Spirit. He is self-existent, eternal, unchanging, omnipotent (all powerful), omniscient (all knowing), and omnipresent (present everywhere).

Second, the Bible is the God-inspired, infallible, and inerrant Word of God.

Third, humans are physical and spiritual beings created by God in His image.

Fourth, because of sin, all of humankind has lost the possibility of having the relationship with God that Adam and Eve enjoyed in the Garden of Eden. Therefore, all are in need of a redeeming savior.

Fifth, Jesus Christ, the second person of the Trinity, the Son of God, came to earth and was born in human flesh to a virgin. He then lived a sinless life and was unjustly crucified on a cross to take the judgment (which is death) due to all who have sinned. Three days later, He rose from the dead. If we surrender our lives (by faith) to Jesus's lordship (controlling direction), we can obtain eternal life. This very same Jesus will come to Earth again to judge the world and deliver His people (the Church.)

Sixth, the Church is God's ordained (sanctioned) representative on Earth. It is composed of all Christian believers (aka God's people). When believers meet together, the church is the sanctioned place for worship, fellowship, administering communion and baptism, discipling, and evangelizing the world.

I hope as you continue on your journey to discovering the gospel according to you, you will see the importance of both scripture and tradition in discovering it.

We will now explore the importance of experience in our search for understanding.

Experience

We have seen the importance of scripture and tradition in developing our personal understanding of what is the Gospel. It is now time to explore how experience figures into this truth-exploring journey we are on.

The longer we live our lives with God as our guide, the more we learn to discern truth from falsity. Therefore, our daily lives serve as a great laboratory to prove what we believe is true. By living it out, we can find out if our truth matches up to "the spiritual sniff test." I like what Larry Osborne, the author of *Ten Dumb Things Smart Christians Believe: Are Urban Legends & Sunday School Myths Ruining Your Faith?*, has to say about this. He postulates that we need to continually be asking two basic questions before adopting a principle or truth as the Gospel.

1. How does this idea or teaching match up with the way life really works?
2. How does this idea or teaching match up with what the Bible (not just one verse but the entire Bible) says?[6]

---

[6] Larry Osborne, *Ten Dumb Things Smart Christians Believe: Are Urban Legends & Sunday School Myths Ruining Your Faith?* (Colorado Springs, CO: Multnomah, 2010), 174.

Using these principles will keep our gospel settled on solid ground. An example of how this works is found in the process of translating Romans 8:28. Let's look at how this verse is translated in the King James Version of the Bible.

> And we know that all things work
> together for good to them that love God,
> to them who are the called according to
> his purpose.

Have you noticed that this isn't how life works? Even for the godliest among us, some things in life don't always work out good for us. What's going on here? Is Scripture wrong? No!

This verse obviously fails when we apply the first question above to it. Where do we go from here? We can begin by looking at other versions of the Bible to see if any of them translate this verse differently.

As we begin searching through other translations, we find many that have the exact, or very similar, wording. That's because this verse is "untouchable" for most translators. However, there is one version that dares to offer a different translation: the Revised Standard Version. This is how the verse appears.

> We know that in everything God works
> for good with those who love him, who
> are called according to his purpose.

As you can see with this translation, we find that God is not manipulating all of reality so that things always work out well for us. Rather, it says that God is cooperating with us as we fulfill our purpose of bringing good to all situations. Doesn't this seem to be more in line with reality and, most of all, with what Scripture teaches? I think so. That's why it's part of my gospel. Here is where I have leaned on experience to help me obtain understanding.

In Hebrews 12:1, we read

> Therefore, since we have so great a cloud of witnesses surrounding us, let us also lay aside every encumbrance and the sin which so easily entangles us, and let us run with endurance the race that is set before us.

This verse discusses the great saints of God who have gone before us throughout history and have shown us the way of Christ. However, many living among us right now also possess great wisdom acquired through their long experience of following Christ. It will benefit you immensely to hear what these saints have to say about Christ and His Gospel.

Let us now investigate how reason helps us on our journey of discovering the gospel according to you.

CHAPTER 4

Reason

Now we will explore the place that reason plays in discovering our personal understanding of what the Gospel is.

Some modern theologians feel that reason should not have any bearing on theological development. They believe that faith is not based on reason but on felt experience. However, I am convinced that they are ignoring what scripture has to say in Romans 12:1-2.

> I beseech you therefore brethren, by the mercies of God, that ye present your bodies a living sacrifice, holy, acceptable unto God, which is your reasonable service. And be not conformed to this world: but be ye transformed by the renewing of your mind, that ye may prove what is that good, and acceptable, and perfect, will of God. (KJV)

Here we see that it is our reasonable service to serve God. The Greek word used here for reasonable is λογικὴν *(logiken)* which translated means "logical" or "rational." Scripture seems to tell us that using reason to verify our beliefs in God is warranted. Accordingly, as we think about God's truth, we are transformed in the process.

In addition, many theologians have seen the correlation that reason has with faith. Harry Gensler, retired professor of philosophy, summarizes St. Thomas Aquinas's[1] ideas on this subject as follows.

> "Reason" covers what we can know by experience and logic alone. From reason, we can know that there is a God and that there is only one God; these truths about God are accessible to anyone by experience and logic alone, apart from any special revelation from God. "Faith" covers what we can know by God's special revelation to us (which comes through the Bible and Christian Tradition). By faith, we can know that God came into the world through Jesus Christ and that God is triune (Father, Son, and Holy Spirit). These truths about God cannot be known by reason alone.[7]

According to Aquinas, faith builds on reason. Since faith and reason are both ways of arriving at truth, and since all truths are harmonious with each other, faith is consistent with reason. If we understand faith and reason

---

[7] Harry J. Gensler, "Religion A4: Aquinas—Faith and Reason," Harryhiker, accessed October 20, 2022, http://www.harryhiker.com/re/r-a4--00.htm.

correctly, there will be no conflict between what faith tells us and what reason tells us.

Here we see that the Christian faith is an evidence-based faith, not to be adopted unless one sees evidence that there is a God, His name is Jesus, and He is in the redemption business.

As we continue our journey into the truth about God, it is imperative that we use logic to formulate a basic understanding of His works and His ways. We must also check to see if our ideas are sound. Here a reality check is needed. We must use our brains to sort out which ideas fit with the way things are as we know them and which don't.

In Isaiah 1:18a, God invites us as follows: "Come let us reason together." Here He acknowledges that we can find Him through reason. Let us look at Romans 1:20 to see how this works.

> For since the creation of the world His invisible attributes, His eternal power, and divine nature, have been clearly seen, being understood through what has been made, so that they are without excuse.

In this passage, we see that God acknowledges that humans possess the ability to deduce logically by looking at the creation (earth, stars, sky, and so on) that He, the creator, must exist.

Another example of where the use of reason is necessary for proper biblical interpretation can be seen by interpreting Matthew 5:29–30.

> If your right eye makes you stumble, tear
> it out and throw it from you; for it is better
> for you to lose one of the parts of your
> body, than for your whole body to be
> thrown into Hell.

If one applies reason to this passage, and he or she is aware of God's character, he or she deduces that God does not want needless harm to happen to us. God is not asking us to actually pluck out our eyes or cut off our hands. He is simply emphasizing that sin should be avoided at all costs.

Reason also must be used in situations where there are no scriptural instructions pertaining to the situation. For instance, most Christians believe that abortion and euthanasia are wrong. Why? Because the Bible tells us that we are not supposed to murder. Since it also implicates that a baby is human in the womb, we can reasonably deduce that abortion is wrong in the eyes of God.

Default Scriptures

By using this method, we can develop life-guiding principles and not always need a specific verse to tell us what is right in the sight of God. There are many scriptures that we can use as default scriptures. In lieu of specific ones, they can serve as guides for deciding on correct actions in any given situation.

Micah 6:8 is one of these; it can be used as a default position for many situations. Let's look at it.

He has told you, O man, what is good;
And what does the LORD require of you
But to do justice, to love kindness, and to
walk humbly with your God?

Another great default scripture is Romans 14:23. Here we find a great template for living the Christian life, and a means for making righteous decisions.

But he who doubts is condemned if he eats because his eating is not from faith, and whatever is not from faith is sin.

This passage shows that if we are not convinced that God does not have a problem with our actions, then we should not be doing them.

Another great default passage is Romans 14:13.

Therefore, let us not judge one another anymore, but rather determine this—not to put an obstacle or a stumbling block in a brother's way.

Here we see that the context of the situation we're involved in helps us decide if something we are doing, at the moment, is a good thing to be doing or not.

A part of our gospel discovery is figuring out ahead of time what we believe is the right thing for us to do in these non-absolute situations.

Revelation

We have now looked at the four means of finding gospel understanding contained in the Wesleyan Quadrilateral. These means serve as a great foundation for our journey into discovering truth. However, there are a few more avenues into truth that we need to consider. Let's look at the first, and the most important of all avenues for Christians: revelation.

In Matthew 16:13–18, we read,

> Now when Jesus came into the district of Caesarea Philippi, He was asking His disciples, "Who do people say that the Son of Man is?" And they said, "Some *say* John the Baptist; and others, Elijah; but still others Jeremiah, or one of the Prophets. He said to them, "But who do you say that I am?" Simon Peter answered, "You are the Christ, the Son of the living God." And Jesus said to him, "Blessed are you, Simon Barjona because flesh and blood did not show this to you, but my Father in Heaven. I also say to you that you are Peter, and upon this rock, I will build My

> church; and the gates of Hades will not overpower it."

Throughout church history, this verse has generally signaled that the "rock" on which the Church is to be built is Peter. However, because of study into the original language and the context found here, I believe that the "rock" the Church is built upon is the revelation that Jesus is the Christ, the Son of the living God.

Let's explore this further. The Greek word used here for Peter is *Petros*, which means "little rock." However, the word used here for rock is *petra* which means "large rock." Using George Abbott-Smith's *A Manual Greek Lexicon of the New Testament*, Bible Hub explains it like this.

> *Pétros* (a *masculine* noun)—properly, a stone (pebble), such as a small rock found along a pathway...*Pétros* ("small stone") then stands in contrast to...*pétra* ("cliff, boulder."[8]

We can see that the word used for rock in this passage does not refer to Peter but to something else. That something else is the revelation that Christ is the Son of the Living God.

Jesus told His disciples He would reveal things to them that He would show to no others. Let's look at this passage in Luke chapter 8:9–10.

---

[8] "Petros," Bible Hub, accessed October 20, 2022, https://biblehub.com/greek/4074.htm.

His disciples began questioning Him as to what this parable meant. And He said, "To you, it has been granted to know the mysteries of the kingdom of God, but to the rest, it is in parables so that SEEING THEY MAY NOT SEE, AND HEARING THEY MAY NOT UNDERSTAND."

We learn from this passage and others that if we are followers of Christ, we have the privilege of having God reveal to us truths only known by God and His followers.

The most common time to receive direct revelation from our Lord is when we are reading his Word. To that end, we should spend a great amount of time doing that. Therefore, whenever we read scripture or pursue our own understanding of the Gospel, we should pray and ask God to reveal these wonderful truths to us. I personally pray the prayer found in Psalm 119:18: "Open my eyes, that I may behold wonderful things from Your law."

The Greek word for revelation, *apokalypsis*, means "unveiling." This is similar to the introduction of a new statue or iconic bust in a museum; it is covered until the appropriate time when the covering is pulled off to reveal the new creation. In the same way, the Holy Spirit pulls the covering off scripture and the real deep meaning is revealed. As we know from scripture, the Holy Spirit's job is to reveal what Jesus is like to us; that's who our Gospel should reveal to others. The more we do this, the more the Holy Spirit will reveal to us.

It's interesting to note that the last book in the Bible is called "The Revelation of Jesus Christ." It's an entire book written to reveal who Jesus is. This is also the main reason the Holy Spirit is at work today: to reveal who Christ is to us. Thus, our gospel message must also have this primary purpose of revealing Jesus to others.

The important thing to remember about anything God reveals to us is this: it needs to be obeyed, if that is required by Him, and also used responsibly. We must not allow these secrets that God tells us to make us prideful or lazy in our pursuit of Him or His truth. The principle here is that when we obey the light (knowledge) we have been given (revealed), we will be given more. If we don't, we won't.

CHAPTER 6

Telling Them

If you have been using the principles and processes enumerated in this book, you should be well on your way to discovering your unique gospel. Now it's time to tell others about it.

There are many resources available to help you with the how-tos of witnessing, so I won't be covering those in this chapter. However, I do have some principles to share here that I believe are essential for a successful witnessing encounter.

1. You want to leave the Gospel recipient with a positive and accurate view of what God is like.
2. You should leave this person desiring to make contact with a Christian again.
3. Hopefully, you can also leave the recipient uncomfortable with living in an ungodly manner.

These goals are based on the idea that it takes many encounters with Christians before the average person makes a serious commitment to Christ. As the Scriptures tell us, some sow the seed, some water, but God gives the increase (1 Corinthians 3:7–9 NLT).

As I mentioned previously, I will not be illustrating a

lot of witnessing methods here. However, I believe that it's advantageous to look at how Jesus did it.

The story of Jesus's encounter with the Samaritan woman at the well serves as an excellent template for all one-on-one verbal evangelistic situations. Let's look at it in John 4:5–26.

> So He came to a city of Samaria called Sychar, near the parcel of ground that Jacob gave to his son Joseph; and Jacob's well was there. So, Jesus, being wearied from His journey, was sitting thus by the well. It was about the sixth hour.
>
> There came a woman of Samaria to draw water. Jesus said to her, "Give Me a drink." For His disciples had gone away into the city to buy food. Therefore, the Samaritan woman said to Him, "How is it that You, being a Jew, ask me for a drink since I am a Samaritan woman?" (For Jews have no dealings with Samaritans.) Jesus answered and said to her, "If you knew the gift of God, and who it is who says to you, 'Give Me a drink,' you would have asked Him, and He would have given you living water." She said to Him, "Sir, you have nothing to draw with and the well is deep; where then do You get that living water? You are not greater than our father Jacob, are You, who gave us the well, and drank of it himself and his sons and his cattle?"

Jesus answered and said to her, "Everyone who drinks of this water will thirst again; but whoever drinks of the water that I will give him shall never thirst, but the water that I will give him will become in him a well of water springing up to eternal life." The woman said to Him, "Sir, give me this water, so I will not be thirsty nor come all the way here to draw."

He said to her, "Go, call your husband and come here." The woman answered and said, "I have no husband." Jesus said to her, "You have correctly said, 'I have no husband'; for you have had five husbands, and the one whom you now have is not your husband; this you have said truly." The woman said to Him, "Sir, I perceive that You are a prophet. Our fathers worshiped in this mountain, and you people say that in Jerusalem is the place where men ought to worship." Jesus said to her, "Woman, believe Me, an hour is coming when neither in this mountain nor in Jerusalem will you worship the Father"…"You worship what you do not know; we worship what we know, for salvation is from the Jews. But an hour is coming, and now is, when the true worshipers will worship the Father in spirit and truth; for such people the Father seeks to be His worshipers. God is

> spirit, and those who worship Him must worship in spirit and truth." The woman said to Him, "I know that Messiah is coming (He who is called Christ); when that One comes, He will declare all things to us." Jesus said to her, "I who speak to you am He."

Let's take a close look at Jesus's approach to this woman. First, He asks her for some water. This would normally not happen because He is a Jew and she is a Samaritan. As stated here, in that day Jews didn't associate with Samaritans, but Jesus shows that He's not concerned with these societal rules. With this gesture, He shows this woman that she is valuable to Him. This is our first task: let the person we're talking to feel that we value and care about him or her. The saying "People don't care how much you know until they know how much you care" rings true here.

Next, He introduces the provocative idea of "living water." This immediately makes her curious about this unusual water and Him. When witnessing, it helps to make the person curious about our message and who we are. For example, you can ask, "Have you ever met someone from the Kingdom of Yahweh?" (Yahweh is a Hebrew name for God used in the Old Testament.)

Following this, he asks her to go get her husband, already aware, using inside information given to Him through a "word of knowledge"[2] that she doesn't have one. He knows she has already had five and is currently living with a man out of wedlock. Being Spirit-filled[3] and depending on the Holy Spirit to give us insight into the life of the person we are communicating with is essential to successful witnessing.

After this, Jesus presents the Gospel, uniquely tailored to this woman, in such a way to allow her to conclude through her own reasoning that He is the Messiah. This is great witnessing! This is the process to use if we want to be successful witnesses: allow the Gospel recipient to think his or her way to truth. This is accomplished by asking leading questions and listening carefully. By listening, you earn the right to speak.

The following summarizes these witnessing principles.

1. Be friendly and caring with your Gospel recipient;
2. Ask leading questions about what he or she believes;
3. Listen carefully;
4. Tell the person the Gospel according to you;
5. Gently answer his or her objections and questions; and
6. If the person is ready and receptive, lead him or her to a commitment to Christ.

Finally, all of the processes above must be accompanied by and followed up with prayer. We must always remember that it is God who saves people, not us.

Finally...

In John 8:31–32, we read the following.

> So, Jesus was saying to those Jews who had believed Him, "If you continue in My word, then you are truly disciples of Mine; and you will know the truth, and the truth will make you free."

We have now reached the end of this book but, hopefully, not your journey into your ongoing unique gospel discovery. As you can see from the passage above, discovering truth is a lifelong quest. However, our reward is that, as we continue to pursue truth, God is creating freedom in us.

Although your journey into God's truth should continue, if you have been diligent in your study, prayer, practice, and sharing of the gospel truth to this point you may have already discovered what you would define as the gospel according to you. If so, here are three questions to help confirm that you have.

1. Does your unique understanding of the gospel cause you to love Jesus more?

2. Is your gospel scripturally accurate?
3. Is this the gospel that you will die for?

If so, then it's time to preach it, live it, defend it, and if necessary, die for it!

May God always be with you as you do!

Bibliography

"Context." Oxford Learner's Dictionaries. Accessed October 19, 2022. https://www.oxfordlearnersdictionaries.com/us/definition/english/context.

Cooper, Dr. David L. "The Golden Rule of Interpretation." *Hermeneutics: The Science of Interpreting the Scriptures.* The Association of Messianic Congregations. Accessed October 19, 2022. http://www.messianicassociation.org/ezine19-dc.hermeneutics.htm.

Gensler, Harry J. "Religion A4: Aquinas—Faith and Reason." Harryhiker. Accessed October 20, 2022. http://www.harryhiker.com/re/r-a4--00.htm.

Kynes, William L. "The Science and Art of Interpretation." *How to Read the Bible.* Podcast audio. March 27, 2021. https://www.cslewisinstitute.org/resources/knowing-doing-podcast-how-to-read-the-bible-part-2-the-science-and-art-of-interpretation/.

Osborne, Larry. *Ten Dumb Things Smart Christians Believe: Are Urban Legends & Sunday School Myths Ruining Your Faith?* Colorado Springs, CO: Multnomah, 2010.

"Thomas Aquinas." Wikipedia. Last updated October 20, 2022. https://en.wikipedia.org/wiki/Thomas_Aquinas.

Endnotes

1 According to Wikipedia, "Thomas Aquinas…was an Italian Dominican friar and priest, who was an immensely influential philosopher, theologian, and jurist in the tradition of scholasticism; he is known within the scholastic tradition as the *Doctor Angelicus*, the *Doctor Communis*, and the *Doctor Universalis*."

2 "Word of knowledge" is one of the gifts of the Spirit mentioned in 1 Corinthians 12:8.

3 Being Spirit-filled, as used here, means that you have been endowed with "power from on high" (Luke 24:49) and that you regularly use the gifts enumerated in 1 Corinthians 12:7–10.

Printed in the United States
by Baker & Taylor Publisher Services